Some Grimm Fairy Tales

Written by
Jill Atkins

Illustrated by
Victor Tavares

Published in 2026 by
Norwood House Press
2544 Clinton Street
Buffalo, NY 14224

Photograph of the brothers Grimm page 5 taken by Hermann Biow in 1847.
Photograph of Hans Christian Andersen page 15 taken by Thora Hallager, at Kongens Nytorv in Copenhagen, in October 1869.

Printed in the United States of America

Library of Congress Cataloging-in-Publication Data:
Names: Atkins, Jill (Children's author). | Tavares, Victor, illustrator.
Title: Some Grimm fairy tales / written by Jill Atkins, illustrated by Victor Tavares. Mystery of Nazca Lines / by Jill Atkins.
Description: Buffalo, NY : Norwood House Press, 2026. | Series: Phonics all-stars: phase 5c
Identifiers: ISBN 9781978578562 (pbk.) | ISBN 9781978578579 (library bound) | ISBN 9781978578586 (ebook)
Subjects: LCSH: Reading–Phonetic method–Juvenile literature. | English language–Phonetics–Juvenile literature. | Fairy tales–Juvenile literature. | Folklore–Germany–Juvenile literature. | Nazca Lines Site (Peru)–Juvenile literature
Classification: LCC LB1573.3 A796 2026 | DDC 372.465–dc23

CPSIA compliance information: Batch #CW26NHP: For further information contact Norwood House Press at 1-800-237-9932.

Have you ever seen any of those big-screen movies that are based on fairy tales?

Movies such as *Snow White* or *Cinderella*.

Or you may have heard of these fairy tales from books or plays.

They are bright and fun to read or watch, but they do have some frightening parts.

Many of these stories are based on original fairy tales from long ago.

Some of these stories are based on tales collected by the German brothers, Jacob and Wilhelm Grimm, about 200 years ago.

They put them into books and published them.

Some of the fairy tales they collected include the stories of Little Red Riding Hood, Rapunzel, Hansel and Gretel, and Rumpelstiltskin – as well as Snow White and Cinderella.

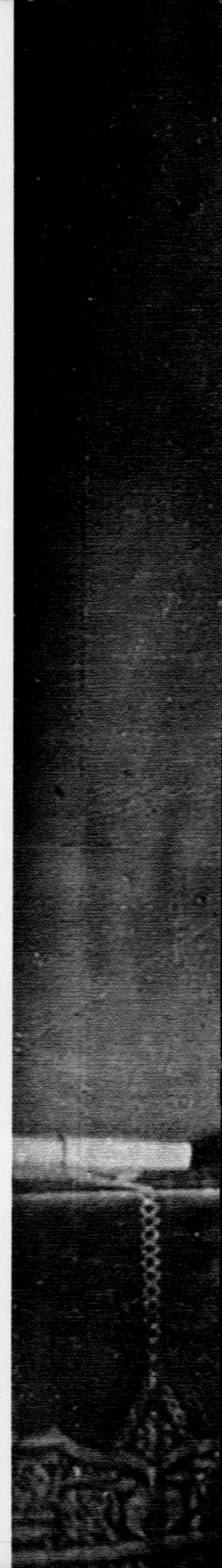

The Grimm brothers

The brothers Grimm told these fairy tales in such a way that many of them were very frightening and gruesome!

Their tales were not really written for children. In fact, the Grimm fairy tales are all quite grim!

For example, in the Grimm brothers' retelling of the French fairy tale of Cinderella, there is no fairy godmother to put Cinderella into a pumpkin coach.

Now this is the grisly part. At the end of the Grimm story, the ugly sisters cut off their toes and heels so their feet would fit into the glass slippers. (Some magic doves see the slippers turn red and tell on the sisters.)

Even worse, their eyes are pecked out by the magic doves.

This is not a story for little children! What were the brothers Grimm thinking?

This is another awful tale:

In the Grimm brothers' story of Snow White, the Wicked Queen was nearly as bad.

She ordered her huntsman to kill Snow White and bring back her lungs and liver, so the queen could eat them.

Luckily for Snow White, the huntsman didn't follow orders!

Can you remember – did they include this in the movie? (Hint: no!)

When filmmakers or writers decided to make these fairy tales into movies, stories, or plays for smaller children, they needed to make them less terrifying.

They still kept some of the danger of the original story, but put some extra magic in to make them perfect for little children to watch.

Not all fairy tales are as horrific.

Hans Andersen, a storyteller from Denmark, wrote playful tales like "The Emperor's New Clothes," "The Ugly Duckling," and "The Little Mermaid."

Andersen's story "The Snow Queen" was turned into the popular movie, *Frozen*.

Andersen's stories were nowhere near as frightening as those of the brothers Grimm.

Hans Andersen

Why do you think the Grimm brothers made their stories so frightening?

The Mystery of the Nazca Lines

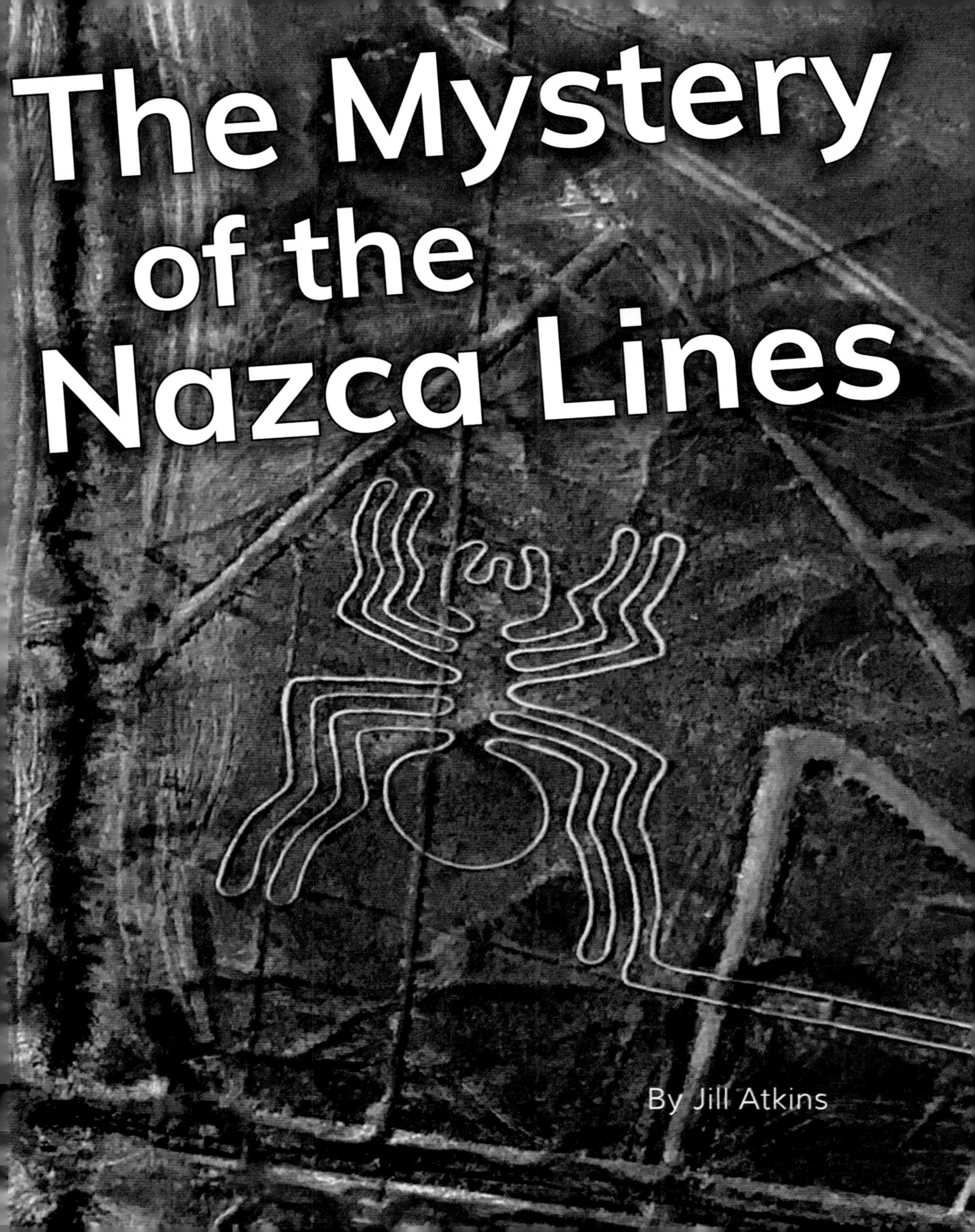

By Jill Atkins

If you visit the hot, dry Nazca Desert in South America, you will see something very strange.

There are lines, pictures, and shapes drawn on the ground.

They are very large. Some of the pictures are over 1,000 feet long.

Who made these lines? When did they make them – and how? What kinds of pictures did they draw – and why?

There are so many mysteries, but what do we really know?

Who made them – and how?

The surface of the Nazca Desert is covered with tiny, dark stones.

About 2,000 years ago, people were living in this desert. We call them the Nazca people.

They scraped away the dark, top layer of stones, revealing a lighter layer below.

In this way, they could make lines and pictures on the ground.

What did they draw?

The Nazca people drew long lines in the desert and made shapes and pictures too. We call these Nazca Lines geoglyphs.

There are hundreds of long lines, drawn on the ground. Each line is about a foot wide, but some of these lines are 30 miles long!

What kinds of pictures did they draw?

The best-known Nazca Lines are the ones that make pictures of animals and plants.

Some of these pictures are massive. This hummingbird is nearly 300 feet long!

How do you draw something so big when you cannot see it from above?

This spider is very well known.

Other creatures the Nazca people drew include a monkey, a whale, a duck, a flower, a tree, and a lizard.

How did a desert people know about whales?

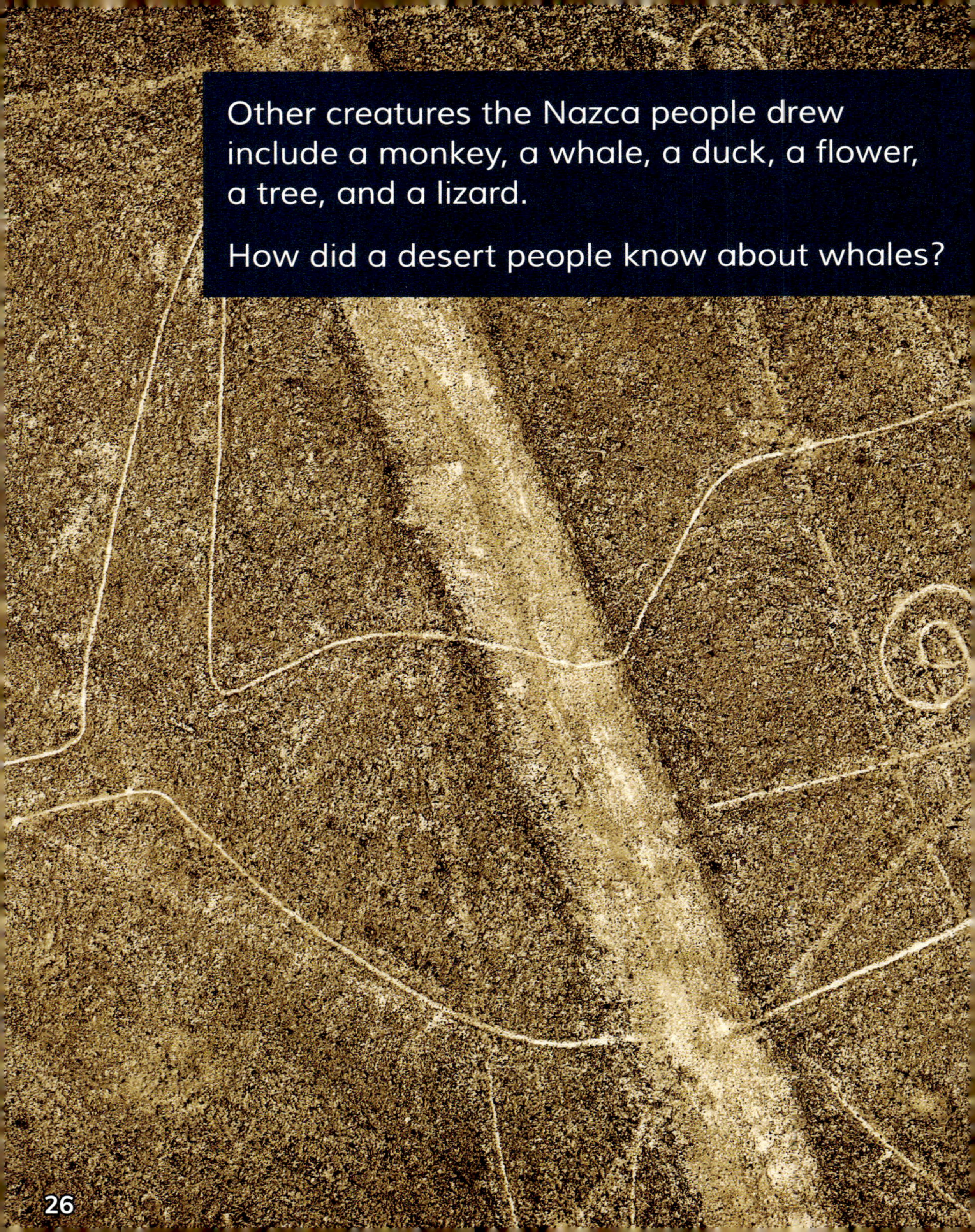

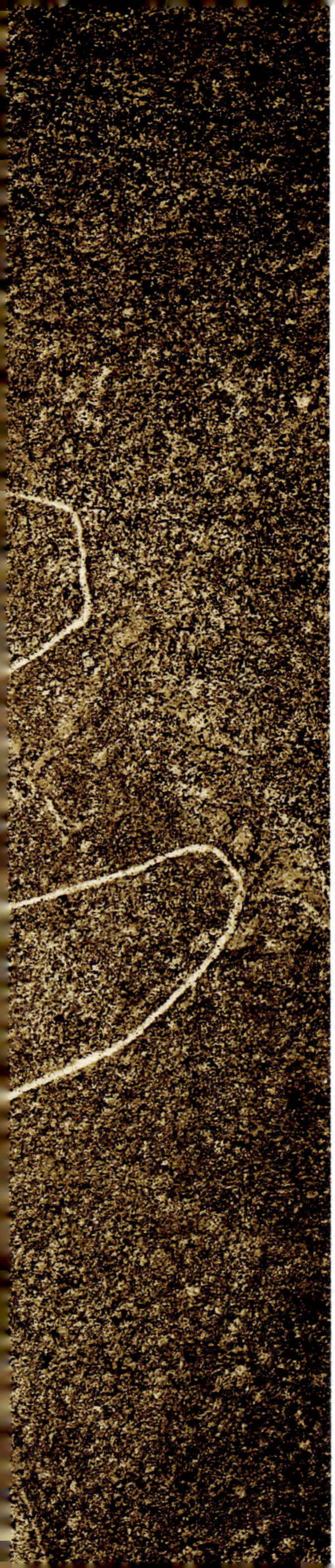

This picture has generated lots of interest. It looks like a human being.

Why did they make them?

The Nazca Lines are a mystery.

We know when they were drawn, but no one knows why.

Some people say that the Nazca people drew them to make their gods happy.

Or were they maps of the stars in the sky, like a calendar?

One man even said that the lines were landing sites for creatures from outer space! (He wrote a book about it.)

He said that the picture on page 27 is of a visitor from space. Do you believe that?

In recent years, people have found other geoglyphs nearby. These are even older than the Nazca Lines.

We call them the Palpa glyphs.

Nearly 100 years ago, people started to fly over the Nazca Desert. That was when they really saw the Nazca Lines in all their glory.

Now people think that there are many more lines under the desert surface, just waiting to be discovered.

Maybe, one day, we will solve this age-old mystery.